E S T A T E   P U B L

REIGATE · MOLE V

DORKING · EPSOM · LEATHERHEAD

G000253239

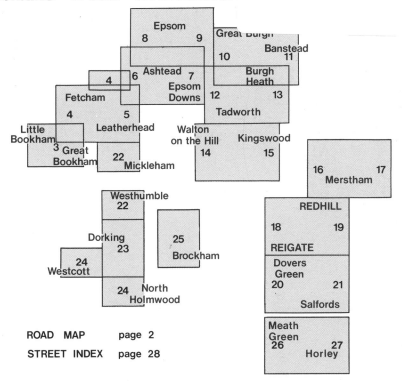

ROAD   MAP   page 2
STREET INDEX   page 28

Every effort has been made to verify
the accuracy of information in this
book but the publishers cannot accept
responsibility for expense or loss
caused by an error or omission.
Information that will be of assistance
to the user of the maps will be welcomed.

The representation on these maps of a
road, track or path is no evidence of the
existence of a right of way.

Car Park	**P**
Public Convenience	**C**
Place of Worship	✚
One-way Street	→
Pedestrianized	▨
Post Office	●

Scale of street plans 4 inches to 1 mile
Unless otherwise stated

Street plans prepared and published by ESTATE PUBLICATIONS, Bridewell House, TENTERDEN, KENT.
The Publishers acknowledge the co-operation of the local authorities
of towns represented in this atlas.

Ordnance Survey® This product includes mapping data licensed from Ordnance Survey®
with the permission of the Controller of Her Majesty's Stationery Office.

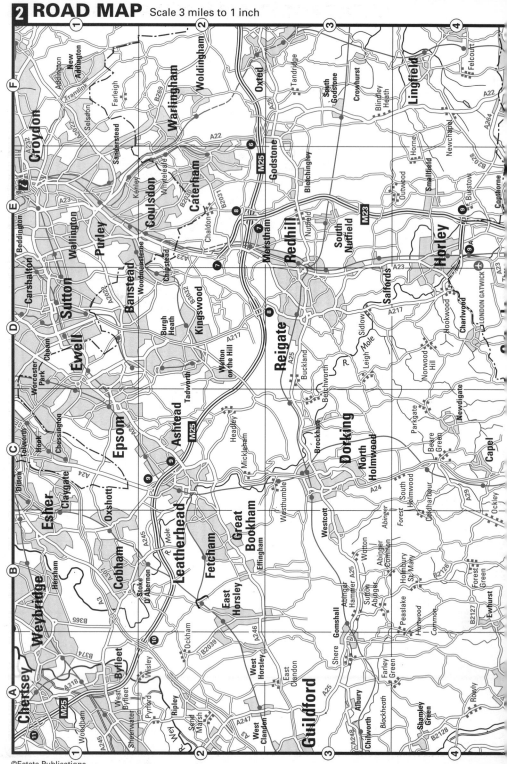

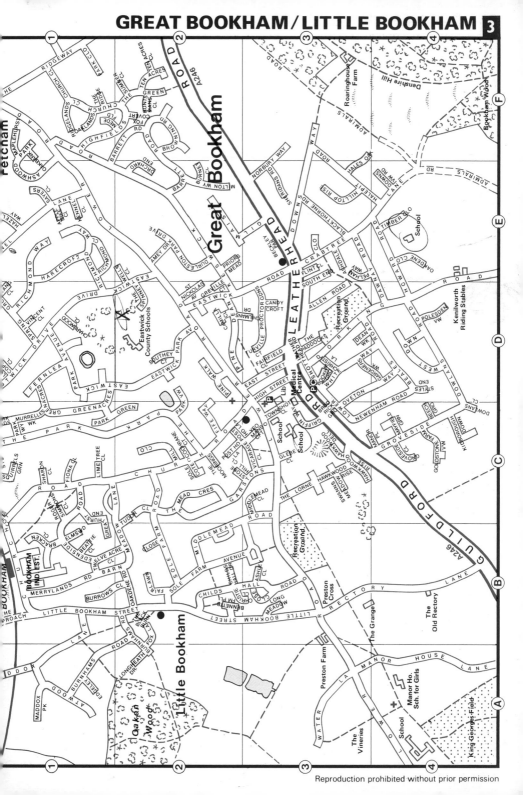

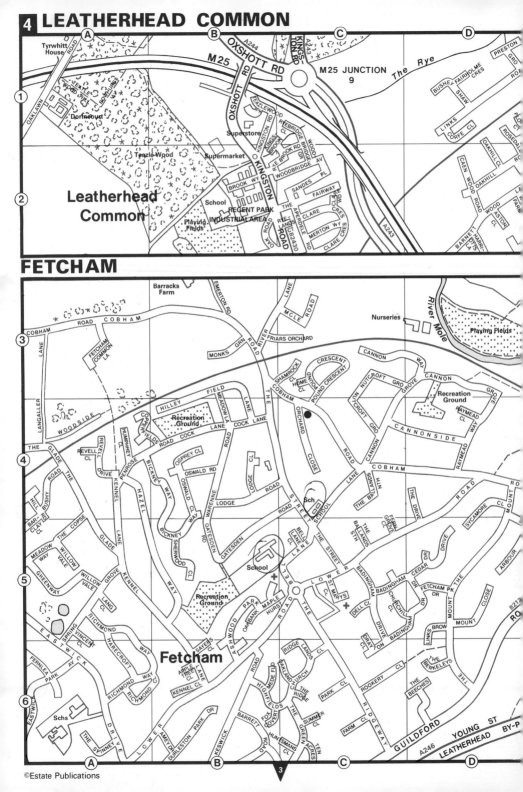

4 LEATHERHEAD COMMON

FETCHAM

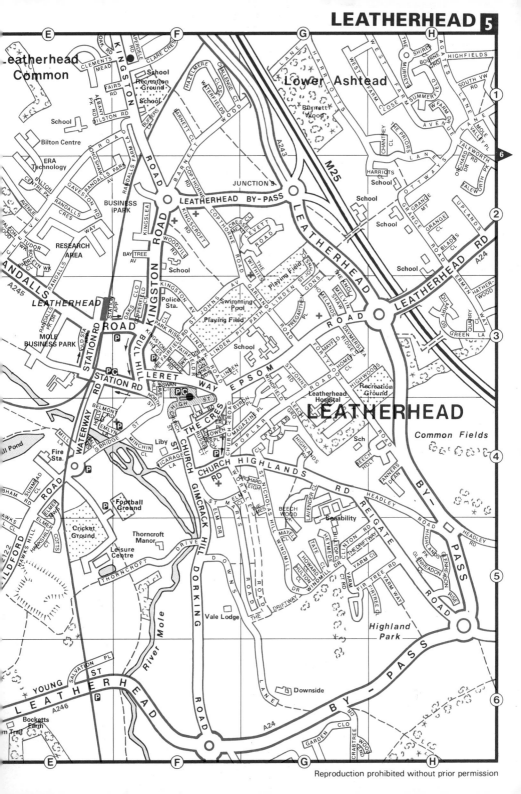

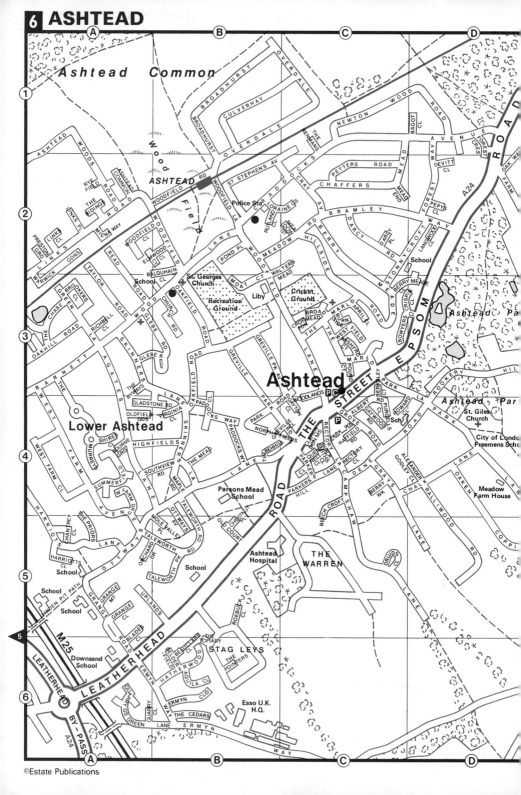

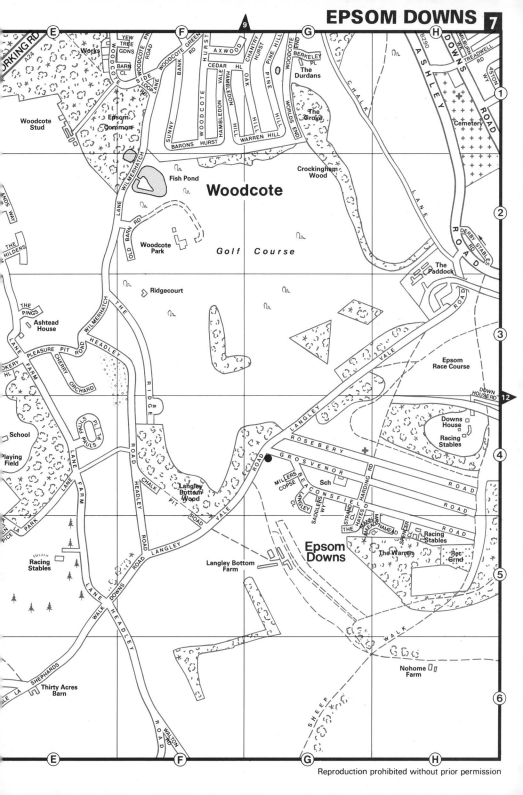

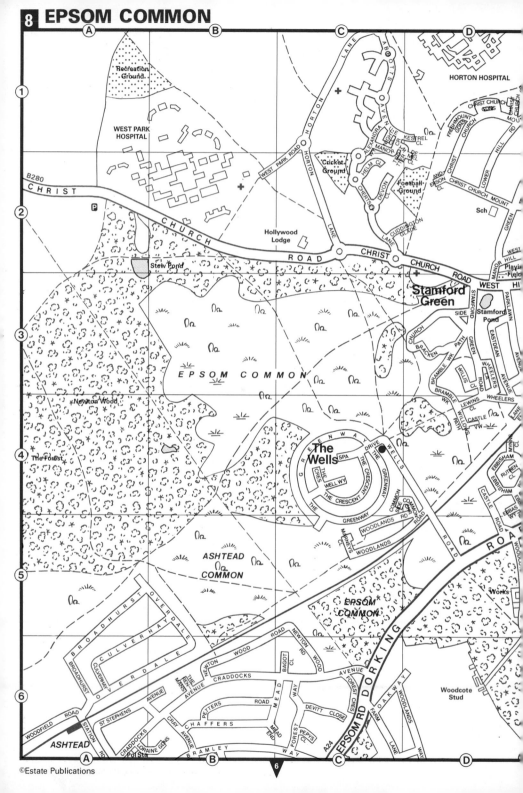

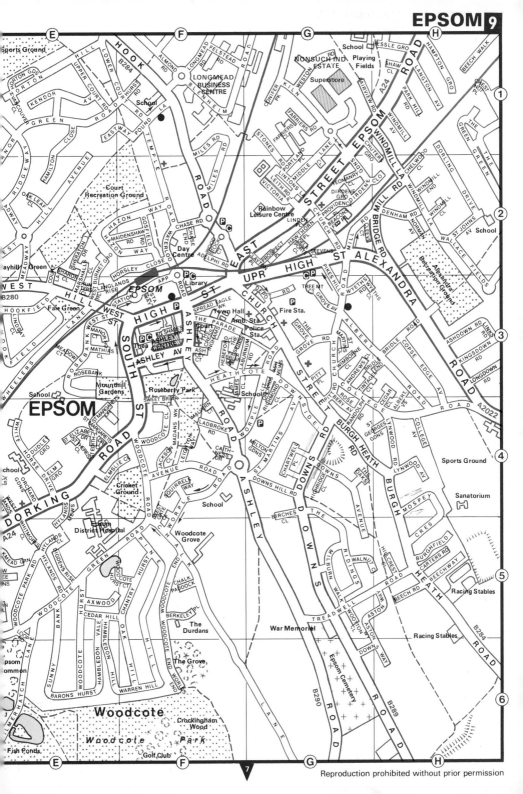

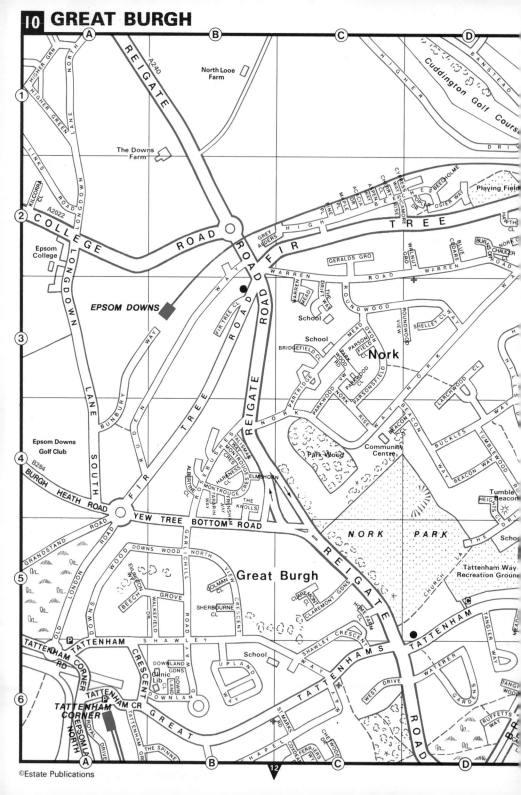

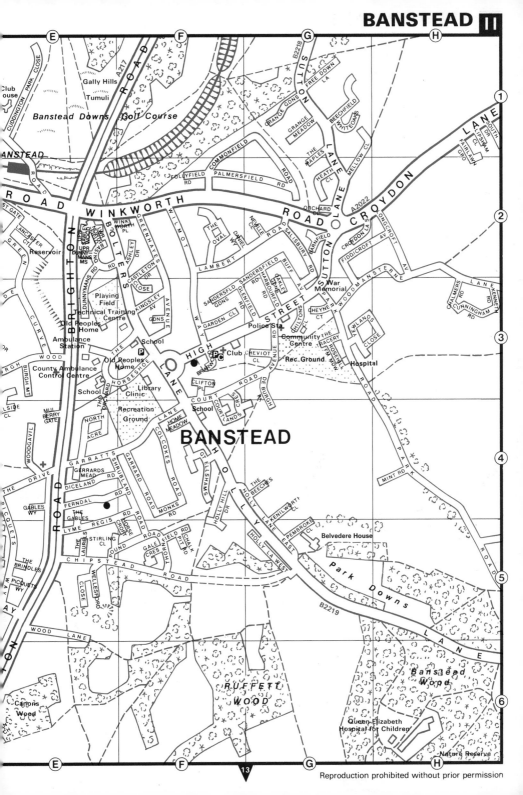

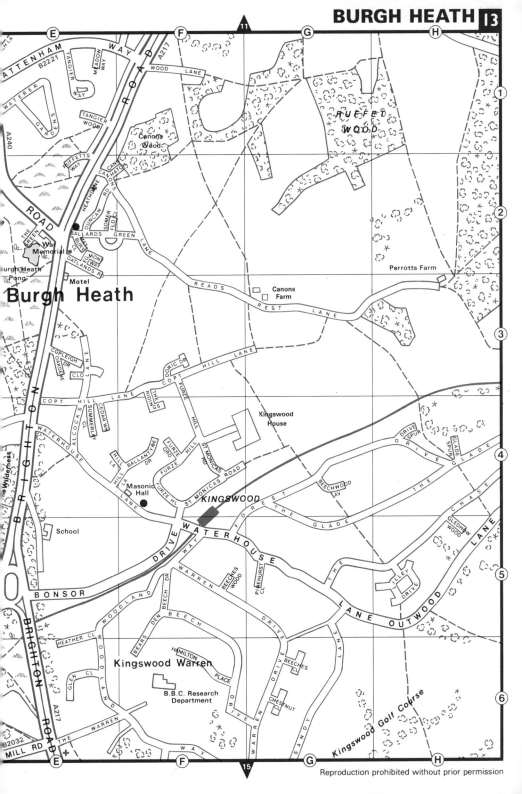

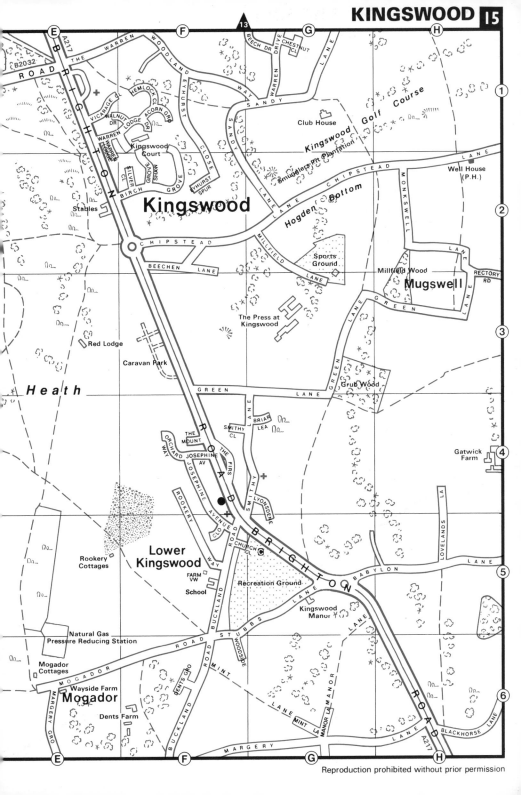

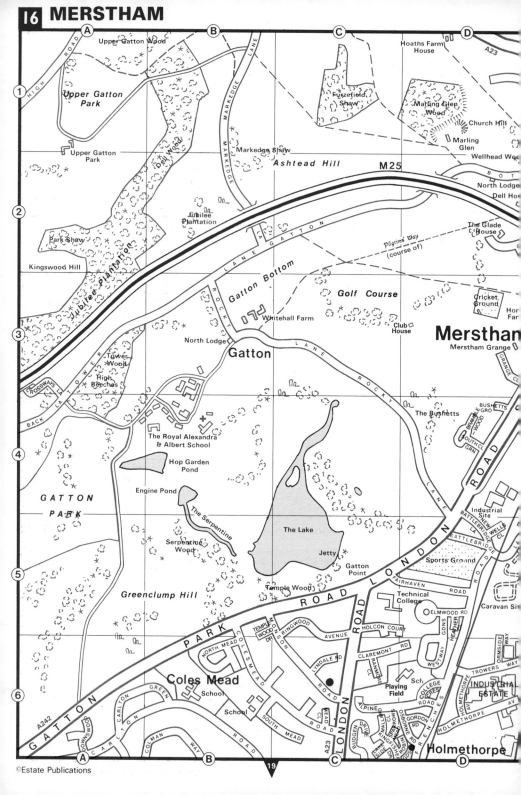

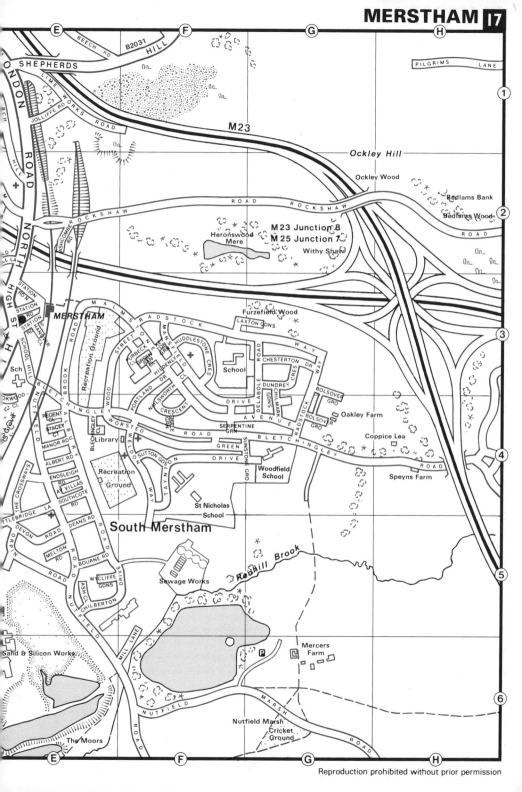

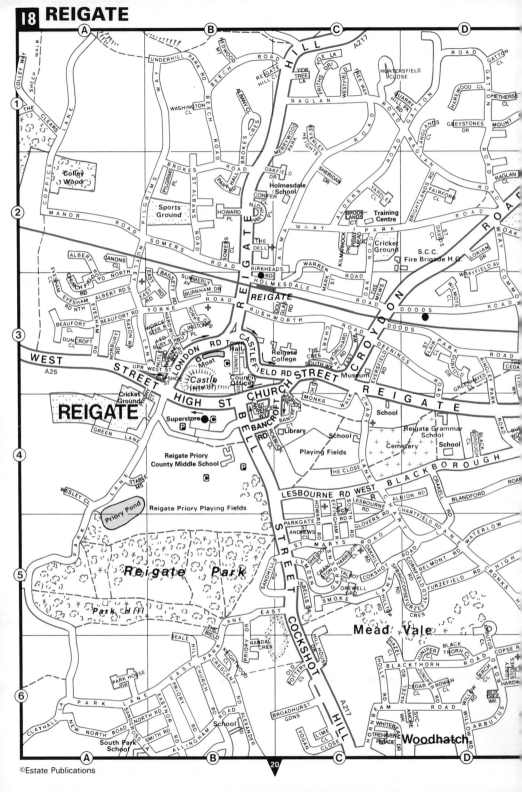

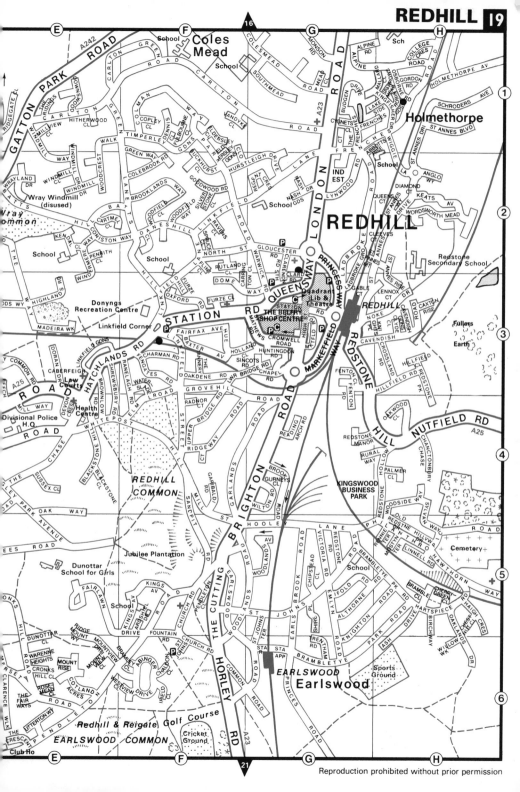

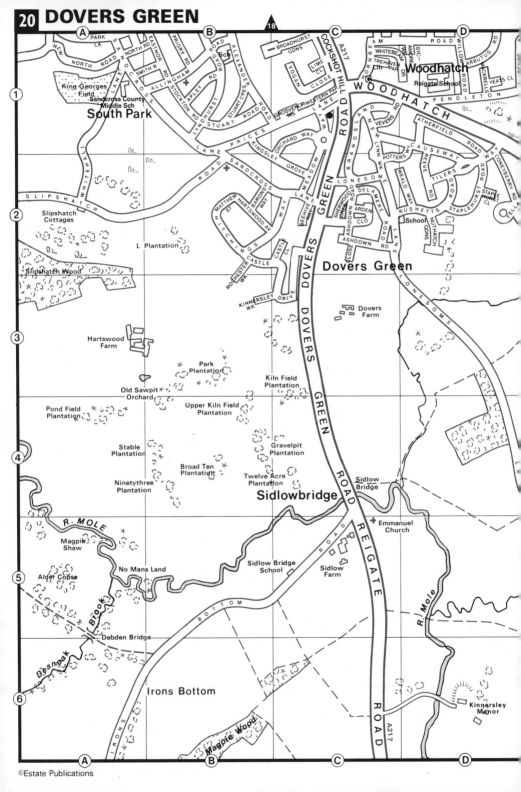

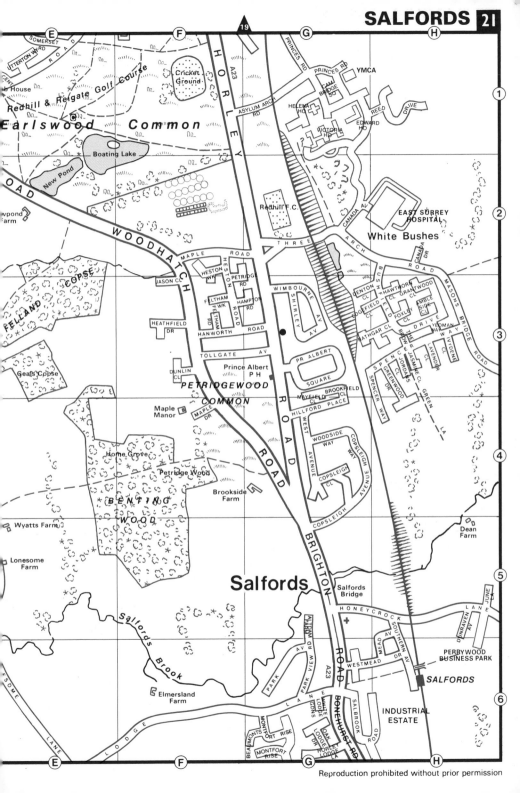

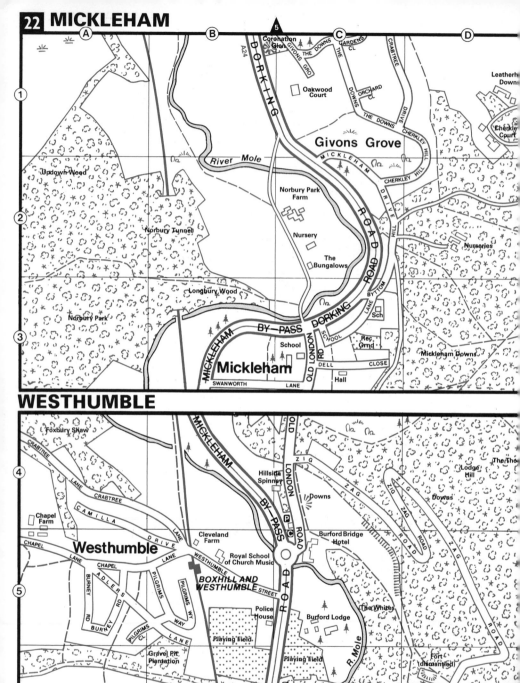

WESTHUMBLE

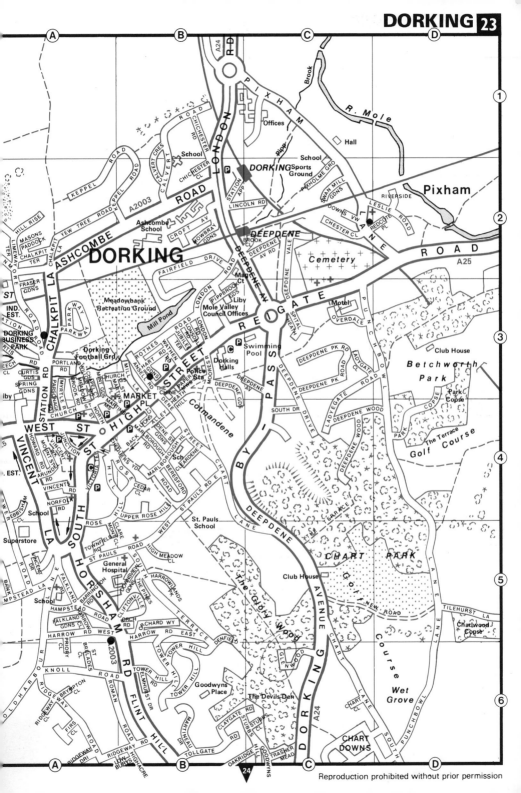

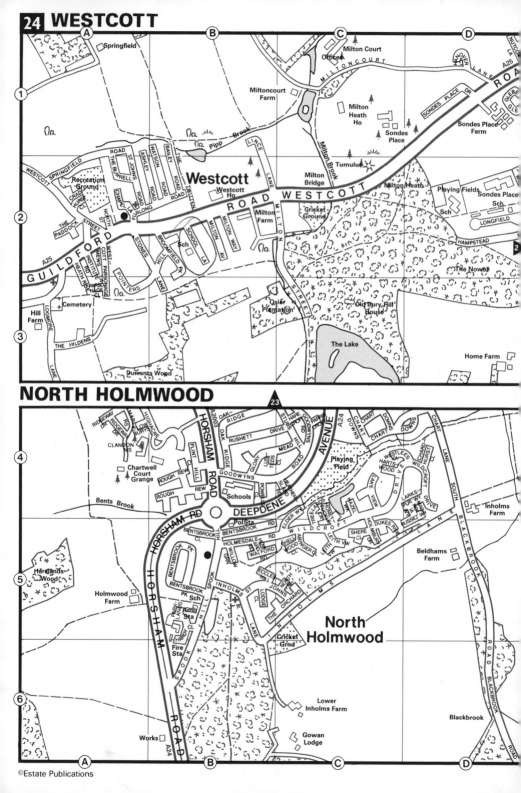

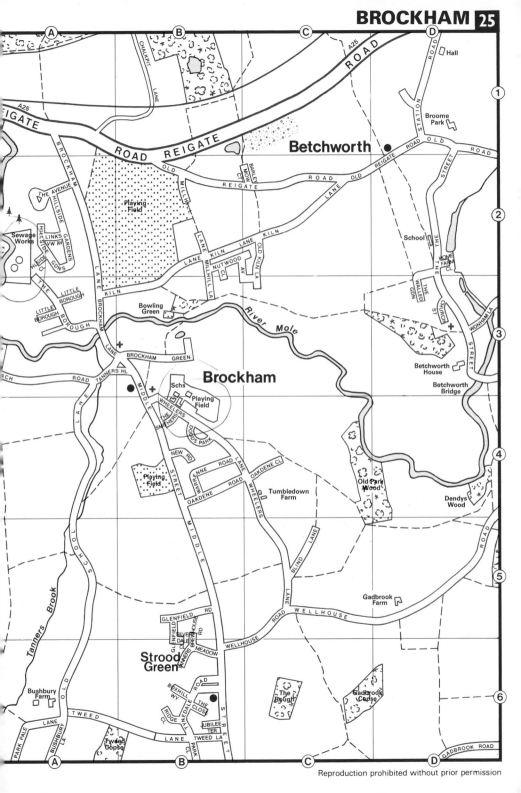

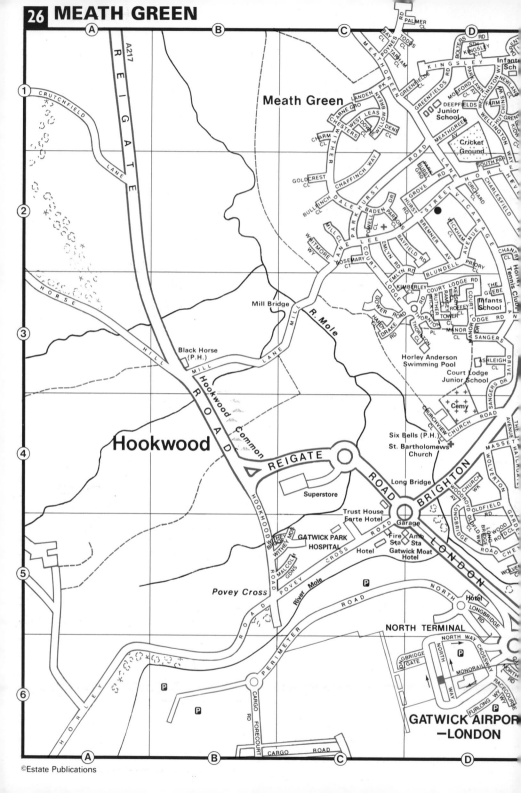

Meath Green

Hookwood

Mill Bridge

R. Mole

Black Horse (P.H.)

Hookwood Common

REIGATE

Superstore

Six Bells (P.H.)
St. Bartholomews Church

Horley Anderson Swimming Pool

Court Lodge Junior School

Cemy

Long Bridge

BRIGHTON

Trust House Forte Hotel

Garage

GATWICK PARK HOSPITAL

Fire Sta

Amb Sta

Gatwick Moat Hotel

Hotel

Povey Cross

River Mole

ROAD

LONDON

Hotel

NORTH TERMINAL

GATWICK AIRPORT—LONDON

Junior School

Cricket Ground

Infants School

Infants School

Hove Tennis Club

THE GLEBE

©Estate Publications

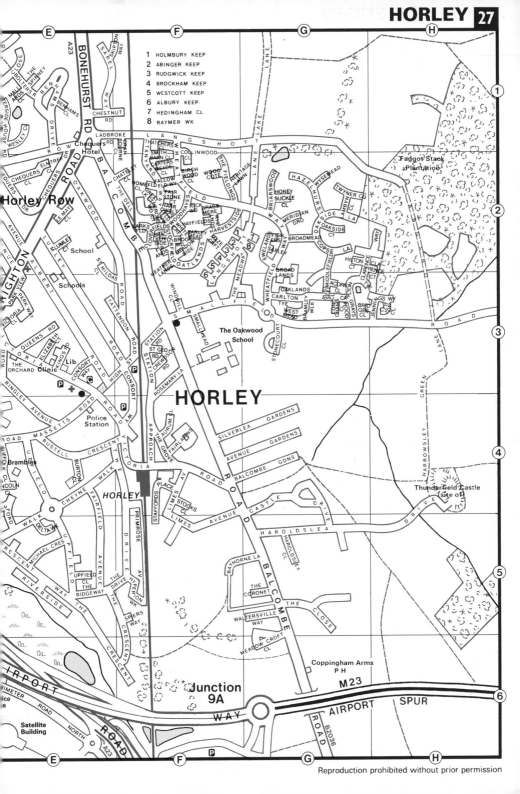

1 HOLMBURY KEEP
2 ABINGER KEEP
3 RUDGWICK KEEP
4 BROCKHAM KEEP
5 WESTCOTT KEEP
6 ALBURY KEEP
7 HEDINGHAM CL
8 RAYMER WK

Faggot Stack Plantation

Horley Row

The Oakwood School

HORLEY

Thunderfield Castle (site of)

Brambles

Police Station

HORLEY

Coppingham Arms PH

Junction 9A

M 23

AIRPORT SPUR

Satellite Building

The Index includes some names for which there is insufficient space on the maps. These names are preceded by an * and are followed by the nearest adjoining thoroughfare.

Troy Clo. KT20 12 B3
Tudor Clo. SM7 11 E3
Tulyar Clo. KT20 12 C3
Tumblewood Rd. SM7 10 D4
Upland Way. KT18 10 B6
Upper Dunnymans Mews. SM7 11 E2
Upper Sawley Wood. SM7 11 E2
Vernon Walk. KT20 12 D3
Vicarage Clo. KT20 15 E1
Walkefield Dri. KT18 10 A5
*Wallace Fields,
  Higher Green. KT17 10 A1
Walnut Clo. KT20 15 E1
Walnut Gro. SM7 10 D2
Walton St. KT20 14 B2
Warren Dri. KT20 13 F5
Warren Lodge. KT20 15 E1
Warren Lodge Dri. KT20 15 E1
Warren Mead. SM7 10 C3
Warren Rd. SM7 10 B2
Waterer Gdns. KT20 10 D6
Waterfield. KT20 12 C3
Waterfield Grn. KT20 12 C4
Waterhouse La. KT20 13 E4
Watermead. KT20 12 C4
Watts La. KT20 12 D5
Watts Mead. KT20 12 D6
Wellesford Clo. SM7 11 E5
Wessels. KT20 12 D4
West Dri. KT20 10 C6
Whitebeam Way. KT20 12 B4
Whitegate Way. KT20 12 B3
Whiteoaks. SM7 11 G1
Willow Bank Gdns. KT20 12 C5
Wilmot Way. SM7 11 F2
Wilsons. KT20 12 D5
Winkworth Pl. SM7 11 F2
Winkworth Rd. SM7 11 E2
Withybed Corner. KT20 14 B1
Wonford Clo. KT20 14 B3
Wood La. KT20 11 E5
Woodgavil. SM7 11 E4
Woodland Way. KT20 13 E5
Woodmansterne La. SM7 11 G3
Woodside. KT20 15 F6
Yew Tree Bottom Rd. KT17 10 A4
Yewlands Clo. SM7 11 G3

EPSOM & ASHTEAD AREA

Abbotts Av. KT198 8 C1
Adelphi Rd. KT19 9 F2
Agates La. KT21 6 A3
Albert Rd. KT21 6 C4
Albert Rd. KT17 9 G3
Albert Villas. KT17 9 H4
Alexander Godley Clo. KT21 6 D4
Alexandra Rd. KT17 9 F3
Alexandra Way. KT19 8 C1
Almond Rd. KT19 9 F1
Anderson Clo. KT19 8 D2
Andrews Clo. KT17 9 G3
April Clo. KT21 6 C3
Aquila Clo. KT21 6 B6
Ash Mews. KT17 9 G3
Ashdown Rd. KT17 9 H3
Ashley Av. KT18 9 F3
Ashley Ct. KT18 9 F3
Ashley Rd. KT18 9 F3
Ashtead Common. KT21 6 A2
Ashtead Woods Rd. KT21 6 A1
Aston Way. KT18 9 H5
Avenue Rd. KT18 9 F4
Axwood. KT18 9 E5
Bagot Clo. KT18 6 D1
Balquhain Clo. KT21 6 B2
Barn Clo. KT18 9 E5
Barnett Wood La. KT21 6 A3
Barons Hurst. KT18 9 E6
Beaconsfield Pl. KT17 9 G2
Beaconsfield Rd. KT18 7 G4
Beauclare Clo. KT22 6 B6
Beech Croft. KT21 6 C4
Beech Rd. KT18 9 H5
Beech Walk. KT17 9 H1
Beechway. KT17 9 H5

Berkeley Ct. KT21 6 C3
Berkeley Pl. KT18 9 F5
Berry Meade. KT21 6 C2
Berry Meade Clo. KT21 6 C2
Berry Walk. KT21 6 C4
Birches Clo. KT18 9 G4
Blacksmiths Clo. KT21 6 C4
Blades Clo. KT21 6 A5
Blenheim Rd. KT19 9 F1
Bourne Gro. KT21 6 A4
Bowyers Clo. KT21 6 C3
Bracken Path. KT18 8 D3
Bramble Walk. KT18 8 D3
Bramley Way. KT21 6 C2
Bridge Rd. KT17 9 H2
Bridle End. KT17 9 H3
Bridle Rd. KT17 9 H3
Broad Mead. KT21 6 C3
Broadhurst. KT21 6 B1
Brookers Clo. KT21 6 A3
Bucknills Clo. KT18 9 F3
Burgh Heath Rd. KT17 9 G4
Burghfield. KT17 9 H5
Burnet Gro. KT19 9 E3
Burnside. KT21 6 C3
Caithness Dri. KT18 9 F4
Carters Rd. KT17 9 H5
Castle Rd. KT18 8 D4
Castle View. KT18 8 D4
Cedar Clo. KT17 9 H4
Cedar Hill. KT18 9 E5
Chaffers Mead. KT21 6 C2
Chalk La. KT21 6 D4
Chalk La. KT18 9 F5
Chalk Paddock. KT18 9 F5
Chalk Pit Road. KT18 7 F4
Chantrey Clo. KT21 6 A5
Chantry Hurst. KT18 9 F5
Chartwell Pl. KT18 9 G4
Chase End. KT19 9 F2
Chase Rd. KT19 9 F2
Chelwood Clo. KT17 9 H2
Chertsey La. KT19 8 C2
Chestnut Pl. KT17 9 H1
Chestnut Pl. KT17 6 B5
Cherry Orchard. KT21 7 E3
Christ Church Gdns. KT19 8 D1
Christ Church Mount. KT19 8 D2
Christ Church Pl. KT19 8 D1
Christ Church Rd. KT19 8 A2
Church Rd. KT21 6 B3
Church Rd. KT21 9 G3
Church Side. KT18 8 D3
Church St. KT17 9 G3
Chuters Gro. KT17 9 G1
Clarendon Mews. KT17 6 C4
Clayton Pl. KT17 9 G2
Cleeve Ct. KT17 9 G2
College Av. KT17 9 H4
College Rd. KT17 9 H4
Common Corner. KT18 8 D4
Common Side. KT18 8 C4
Conifer Pk. KT17 9 G1
Copse Edge Av. KT17 9 H3
Court La. KT19 9 E2
Craddocks Av. KT21 6 B2
Crampshaw La. KT21 6 C4
Cray Av. KT21 6 C2
Crispin Clo. KT21 6 C3
Crofton. KT21 6 C3
Cuddington Glade. KT19 8 A4
Culverhay. KT21 6 B1
Darcy Pl. KT21 6 C2
Darcy Rd. KT21 6 C2
De Mel Clo. KT18 9 D1
Delaporte Clo. KT17 9 G2
Delderfield. KT22 6 B6
Dene Rd. KT21 6 C4
Denham Rd. KT17 9 H2
Depot Rd. KT17 9 H2
Derby Stables Rd. KT18 7 H2
Devitt Clo. KT21 6 D2
Devon Clo. KT19 8 C2
Digdens Rise. KT18 9 E5
Dirdene Clo. KT17 9 G2
Dirdene Gdns. KT17 9 G2
Dirdene Gro. KT17 9 G2
Dorking Rd. KT18 9 E4
Dorling Dri. KT17 9 H2
Down House Rd. KT17 7 H3
Downs Av. KT18 9 G4
Downs Hill Rd. KT18 9 G4
Downs Rd. KT18 9 F5
Downs Rd,
  Epsom. KT18 9 G4

Downs Way. KT18 9 G5
Downside. KT18 9 G3
Druids Clo. KT21 6 C5
Drummond Gdns. KT19 8 D1
Dudley Rd. KT18 9 F4
East St. KT19 9 F2
Eastdean Av. KT18 8 D3
Eastway. KT19 9 F1
Ebbas Way. KT18 8 D4
Ebbisham Rd. KT18 8 D4
Elm Gro. KT18 9 F4
Elmslie Clo. KT18 9 E4
Elmwood Clo. KT21 6 B2
Elmwood Ct. KT21 6 B2
Epsom Rd. KT21 6 B2
Epsom Rd. KT17 9 G1
Ermyn Clo. KT22 6 B6
Ermyn Way. KT22 6 A6
Fairbriar Ct. KT18 9 F3
Fairview Rd. KT17 9 G1
Farm La. KT21 7 E2
Farriers Clo. KT17 9 H4
Farriers Rd. KT17 9 H4
Felstead Rd. KT19 9 F1
Forest Cres. KT21 6 D1
Forest Way. KT21 6 D2
Freshmount Gdns. KT18 8 D1
Gayton Clo. KT21 6 C4
Gaywood Rd. KT21 6 C4
Gladstone Rd. KT21 6 A4
Glebe Rd. KT21 6 A3
Gosfield Rd. KT19 9 F2
Grange Clo. KT22 6 A5
Grange Mount. KT22 6 A5
Grange Rd. KT22 6 A5
Grays La. KT17 6 C4
Green La. KT22 6 C4
Green La. KT21 6 A1
Greenway. KT18 8 C4
Greville Clo. KT21 6 B4
Greville Park Av. KT21 6 B3
Greville Park Rd. KT21 6 B3
Grosvenor Rd. KT18 7 G4
Grove Av. KT17 9 G3
Grove Rd. KT21 6 B4
Grove Rd. KT17 9 G3
Hambledon Hill. KT18 9 E5
Hambledon Vale. KT18 9 E6
Hamilton Clo. KT18 9 E5
Hampton Gro. KT17 9 H1
Harding Rd. KT18 7 G4
Harriotts Clo. KT21 6 A5
Harriotts La. KT21 6 A4
Hatfield Rd. KT21 6 C4
Hatherwood. KT22 6 B6
Hawthorne Pl. KT17 9 G2
Hazon Way. KT19 9 E2
Headley Rd. KT18 7 E3
Heathcote Rd. KT1 9 F3
Helm Clo. KT18 8 C2
Hereford Clo. KT18 9 H1
Hessle Gro. KT17 9 H1
High St. KT19 9 F3
Highfields. KT21 6 A4
Highridge Clo. KT18 9 G4
Hillcrest Clo. KT18 9 H5
Hillside Rd. KT21 6 C2
Hook Rd. KT19 9 F1
Hookfield. KT19 9 E3
Horsley Clo. KT19 9 F2
Horton Gdns. KT19 9 E1
Horton Hill. KT19 9 E1
Horton La. KT19 9 E1
Howard Clo. KT21 6 C4
Hunters Clo. KT19 9 E1
Hurst Rd. KT19 9 E1
Hylands Clo. KT18 9 E3
Hylands Mews. KT18 9 E3
Hylands Rd. KT18 9 E5

INDUSTRIAL & RETAIL:
Longmead Business Centre. KT19 9 G4
Nonsuch Ind Est. KT17 9 G4
Jackson Clo. KT18 9 E4
Kendor Av. KT19 9 E1
Kestrel Clo. KT18 9 D1
Kiln La. KT17 9 G1
King Shades Wk. KT18 9 F3
Kingsdown Rd. KT17 9 H3
Laburnam Rd. KT18 9 F4
Ladbroke Rd. KT18 9 F4
Lane End. KT18 8 D4
Langlands Rise. KT19 9 E3
Langley Clo. KT18 9 F3
Langley Vale Rd. KT18 7 F5
Langton Av. KT17 9 H1
Langwood Clo. KT21 6 D2

Leatherhead By-Pass. KT22 6 A6
Leatherhead Rd. KT22 6 A6
Leighton Way. KT18 9 F4
Leith Rd. KT17 9 G2
Lewins Clo. KT18 8 D4
Linden Pit Path. KT22 6 A5
Linden Pl. KT17 9 G2
Lindsay Clo. KT19 9 E3
Links Clo. KT21 6 A2
Links Pl. KT21 6 A2
Links Rd. KT21 6 A2
Links Rd. KT17 9 H3
Lintons La. KT17 9 G2
Little Orchards. KT18 9 G3
Longdown Rd. KT17 9 H3
Longmead Rd. KT19 9 F1
Loop Rd. KT18 9 E5
Loraine Gdns. KT21 6 B2
Lower Court Rd. KT19 9 E1
Lower Hill Rd. KT19 8 D2
Lynwood Av. KT17 9 H4
Lynwood Rd. KT17 9 H4
Madans Walk. KT18 9 F4
Maidenshaw Rd. KT19 9 F2
Malvern Ct. KT18 9 F4
Mannamead. KT18 7 H5
Mannamead Clo. KT18 7 G5
Manor Cres. KT19 8 C1
Manor Green Rd. KT19 9 E1
Manor House Ct. KT18 9 E3
Maple Rd. KT21 6 B4
Marneys Clo. KT18 8 C5
Marshalls Clo. KT18 9 E3
Mathias Clo. KT18 9 E3
Mead End. KT21 6 C2
Meadow Clo. KT18 9 E3
Meadow Gate. KT21 6 C2
Meadow Rd. KT21 6 B2
Meadway. KT19 9 E2
Middle Clo. KT17 9 G2
Middle La. KT17 9 G2
Miena Way. KT21 6 A2
Milburn Walk. KT19 9 G5
Miles Rd. KT19 9 F2
Mill Rd. KT17 9 G2
Millers Copse. KT18 7 G4
Milton Gdns. KT17 9 G3
Moat Ct. KT17 6 B3
Mole Valley Pl. KT21 6 B5
Mospey Cres. KT17 9 H4
Mynns Clo. KT18 8 D4
Newton Wood Rd. KT21 6 C1
Nightingale Clo..KT19 8 C1
Norman Av. KT17 9 H2
North Fields. KT21 6 B4
Oak Hill. KT18 9 F5
Oak Leaf Clo. KT19 9 E2
Oak Way. KT21 6 D2
Oaken Coppice. KT21 6 D4
Oakfield Rd. KT21 6 B3
Oakhill Rd. KT21 6 A3
Oakmead Grn. KT18 9 E5
Old Barn Rd. KT18 7 F2
Old Ct. KT17 6 B5
Oldfield Gdns. KT21 6 A4
Orchard Dri. KT21 6 A5
Orchard Gdns. KT18 9 E4
Ottways Av. KT18 6 B5
Ottways La. KT21 6 A5
Overdale. KT21 6 B1
Paddocks Clo. KT21 6 B4
Paddocks Way. KT21 6 A4
Park Hill Rd. KT17 9 H1
Park La. KT21 6 C3
Park Rd. KT21 6 B4
Park Walk. KT21 6 C4
Parkers Clo. KT21 6 C4
Parkers Hill. KT21 6 C4
Parkers La. KT21 6 C4
Parklawn Av. KT18 8 D3
Pauls Pl. KT21 7 E4
Pebble La. KT18 7 E6
Pepys Clo. KT21 6 D2
Petters Rd. KT21 6 C2
Pikes Hill. KT17 9 F3
Pine Hill. KT18 9 F5
Pitt Pl. KT17 9 G3
Pitt Rd. KT17 9 G3
Pleasure Pit Rd. KT17 7 E3
Pond Pl. KT21 6 B2
Portland Pl. KT17 9 G1
Pound Ct. KT21 6 B4
Pound La. KT17 9 F1
Preston Gro. KT21 6 A5
Prospect Pl. KT17 9 G2
Providence Pl. KT17 9 G2

Purcells Clo. KT21 6 C4
Quennell Clo. KT21 6 C4
Ralliwood Rd. KT21 6 D4
Randolph Rd. KT17 9 G4
Read Rd. KT21 6 A3
Rectory Clo. KT17 6 C4
Rectory La. KT21 6 C4
Richbell Clo. KT17 6 A3
Richmond Clo. KT18 9 G3
Ridgeway. KT19 9 E2
Roebuck Clo. KT21 6 B5
Rookery Hill. KT17 6 D3
Rosebank. KT18 9 E3
Rosebery Av. KT17 9 G4
Rosebery Rd. KT18 7 G4
*Rosedale,
  Oakhill Rd. KT17 6 A3
Ruthen Clo. KT18 8 D4
Rutland Clo. KT17 6 B2
Rye Field. KT21 6 A2
Saddlers Way. KT18 7 G4
St Edith Clo. KT18 9 E4
St Elizabeth Dri. KT18 9 E4
St Georges Gdns. KT17 9 H4
St James Clo. KT18 9 F3
St Johns Av. KT17 9 H2
St Margarets Dri. KT18 9 E4
St Martins Av. KT18 9 G4
St Martins Clo. KT17 9 G3
St Stephens Av. KT21 6 B2
St Theresa Clo. KT18 9 E4
Sharon Clo. KT19 9 E2
Shaw Clo. KT17 9 H1
Sheep Walk. KT18 7 G6
Shephards Walk. KT18 7 E6
Sheraton Dri. KT19 9 E2
Shires Clo. KT21 6 A4
Skinners La. KT21 6 A3
South St. KT18 9 F3
Southview Rd. KT21 6 B4
Spa Dri. KT18 8 C4
Spencer Clo. KT18 7 H5
Spread Eagle Wk. KT18 9 F3
Squirrels Way. KT18 9 F4
Stag Leys. KT21 6 B6
Stamford Green Rd. KT18 8 D3
Station App. KT19 9 F3
Station Way. KT19 9 F3
Stevens Clo. KT17 9 G2
Stones Rd. KT17 9 G1
Stonny Croft. KT21 6 C2
Strand Clo. KT18 7 G4
Summerfield. KT21 6 A4
Sunnybank. KT18 9 E6
Sweet Briar La. KT18 9 F4
Taleworth Pk. KT21 6 B5
Taleworth Rd. KT21 6 A5
Taylor Rd. KT21 6 A3
Temple Rd. KT19 9 F2
The Byways. KT21 6 B5
The Cedars. KT22 6 B6
The Chase. KT21 6 A3
The Crescent. KT18 8 C4
The Cressingham. KT18 9 F3
The Green. KT17 9 H1
The Greenway. KT18 8 C4
The Grove. KT17 9 G3
The Hayes. KT18 9 G5
The Hilders. KT21 7 E2
The Marld. KT21 6 C3
The Mead. KT21 6 B4
The Murreys. KT21 6 A3
The Oaks. KT18 9 G4
The Parade. KT18 9 F3
The Pings. KT21 7 E3
The Pointers. KT21 6 B6
The Priors. KT21 6 A5
The Renmans. KT21 6 C1
The Ridge. KT21 7 F3
The Ridings. KT21 6 A2
The Ridings. KT21 9 G4
The Spinney. KT21 9 F3
The Street. KT21 6 C4
The Topiary. KT21 6 B6
The Warren. KT21 6 C5
Timberhill. KT21 6 B4
Tintagel Clo. KT17 9 G3
Treadwell Rd. KT18 9 G5
Treemount Ct. KT17 9 G3
Trotter Way. KT19 8 C2
Uplands. KT21 6 B5
Upper Court Rd. KT19 9 E1
Upper High St. KT17 9 G2
Vancouver Clo. KT19 9 E1
Victoria Pl. KT17 9 G2
Virginia Clo. KT21 6 B4

Wallace Fields. KT17 9 H2
Walnut Clo. KT18 9 G5
Walters Mead. KT21 6 B2
Walton Rd. KT18 7 F6
Warren Hill. KT18 9 F6
Warwick Gdns. KT21 6 A3
Waterloo Rd. KT19 9 F2
Well Way. KT18 8 C4
Wells Rd. KT18 8 C4
West Farm Av. KT21 6 A4
West Farm Clo. KT21 6 A4
West Farm Dri. KT21 6 A4
West Field. KT21 6 C3
West Hill. KT19 9 E3
West Hill Av. KT19 9 E2
West Park Rd. KT19 8 C2
West St. KT18 9 E3
Westgate Clo. KT18 9 F4
Westlands Ct. KT18 9 E4
Weston Rd. KT17 9 G1
Wheelers La. KT18 8 D3
White Horse Dri. KT18 9 E4
Whitmores Clo. KT18 9 E5
Willis Clo. KT18 8 D3
Willows Path. KT18 8 D4
Wilmerhatch La. KT18 7 E3
Wimborne Clo. KT17 9 G3
Windmill Av. KT17 9 H1
Windmill Clo. KT17 9 H2
Windmill End. KT17 9 H2
Windmill La. KT17 9 H1
Wishford Ct. KT21 6 C3
Woodcote Clo. KT18 9 F4
Woodcote End. KT18 9 F5
Woodcote Green Rd. KT18 9 E5
Woodcote Hurst. KT18 9 E6
Woodcote Hurst Ct. KT18 9 F5
*Woodcote Mews, Worple Rd. KT18 9 F4
Woodcote Pk Rd. KT18 9 E5
Woodcote Rd. KT18 9 F4
Woodcote Side. KT18 7 E1
Woodfield. KT21 6 B2
Woodfield Clo. KT21 6 A2
Woodfield La. KT21 6 B2
Woodfield Rd. KT21 6 B2
Woodlands. KT21 6 C3
*Woodlands Copse, Ashtead Woods Rd. KT21 6 A1
Woodlands Rd. KT18 8 C5
Woodlands Way. KT18 8 C6
Woodstock Ct. KT19 9 F2
Wootton Clo. KT18 9 G5
Worlds End. KT18 7 G1
Worple Rd. KT18 9 F4
Wyeths Clo. KT17 9 G3
Wyeths Rd. KT17 9 G3
Yeomanry Clo. KT17 9 G2
Yew Tree Gdns. KT18 9 E5

HORLEY

Abinger Keep. RH6 27 F2
Acorn Clo. RH6 27 G3
Airport Way. RH6 27 E6
Albert Rd. RH6 27 E2
Albury Keep. RH6 27 F2
Arne Gro. RH6 26 C1
Ashleigh Clo. RH6 26 D3
Aurum Clo. RH6 27 F4
Avenue Gdns. RH6 27 F4
Avondale Clo. RH6 26 D1
Baden Gro. RH6 26 C2
Bakehouse Rd. RH6 27 E1
Balcombe Gdns. RH6 27 F4
Balcombe Rd. RH6 27 E2
Barley Mead. RH6 27 F2
Bay Clo. RH6 26 C1
Bayfield Rd. RH6 26 C2
Bayhorne La. RH6 27 F5
Benhams Clo. RH6 27 E1
Benhams Dri. RH6 27 E1
Birchwood Clo. RH6 27 F2
Blundell Av. RH6 26 D2
Bolters Rd. RH6 27 E1
Bolters Rd Sth. RH6 26 D1
Bonehurst Rd. RH6 27 E1
Brackenside. RH6 27 F2
Bramley Walk. RH6 27 G3
Bremner Av. RH6 26 D2
Briars Wood. RH6 27 G2
Bridges Clo. RH6 27 G3
Brighton Rd. RH6 26 D4
Broadlands. RH6 27 G2
Broadmead. RH6 27 G2
Brockham Keep. RH6 27 F2
Brookwood. RH6 27 F2
Bullfinch Clo. RH6 26 C2
Burton Clo. RH6 27 E4
Cargo Forecourt Rd. RH6 26 B6
Cargo Rd. RH6 26 B6
Carlton Tye. RH6 27 G3
Carters Meade Clo. RH6 27 F2
Castle Dri. RH6 27 G4
Chaffinch Way. RH6 26 C2
Chantry Clo. RH6 26 D2
Charlesfield Rd. RH6 26 D2
Charm Clo. RH6 26 C1
Chatelet Clo. RH6 27 F2
Chequers Clo. RH6 27 E2
Chequers Dri. RH6 27 E2
Chesters. RH6 26 C1
Chestnut Rd. RH6 27 E1
Cheyne Walk. RH6 26 D5
Church Rd. RH6 26 D4
Church Walk. RH6 26 D4
Churchview Clo. RH6 26 D4
Clarence Ct. RH6 27 H2
Clarence Way. RH6 27 G3
Clifton Clo. RH6 27 H3
Cloverfields. RH6 27 F2
Collingwood Clo. RH6 27 F1
Consort Way. RH6 27 E3
Copse La. RH6 27 G2
Court Lodge Rd. RH6 26 C2
Cranbourne Clo. RH6 27 F1
Crescent Way. RH6 27 E5
Crewdson Rd. RH6 27 F3
Crossway. RH6 26 D6
Crutchfield La. RH6 26 A1
Darenth Way. RH6 26 D1
Deepfields. RH6 26 D1
Delta Walk. RH6 27 E5
Dene Clo. RH6 26 C1
Downe Clo. RH6 26 C1
Drake Rd. RH6 26 C3
Elizabeth Ct. RH6 27 E3
Elmtree Clo. RH6 27 E2
Emlyn Rd. RH6 26 C2
Ewelands. RH6 27 G2
Fairfield Av. RH6 27 E4
Fairlawns. RH6 27 F4
Fairstone Ct. RH6 27 F2
Fallowfield Way. RH6 27 F2
Ferndown. RH6 27 E1
Fieldview. RH6 27 F2
Firlands. RH6 27 F2
Fishers. RH6 27 G2
Furlong Way. RH6 26 D6
Gatwick Way. RH6 26 D6
Goldcrest Clo. RH6 26 C2
Gower Rd. RH6 26 C3
Granary Clo. RH6 27 E1
Grassmere. RH6 27 F2
Grays Wood. RH6 27 G3
Greatlake Ct. RH6 27 F2
Greenfields Clo. RH6 26 C1
Greenfields Rd. RH6 26 D1
Grendon Clo. RH6 26 D1
Grove Rd. RH6 26 D2
Hardy Clo. RH6 26 C3
Haroldslea Clo. RH6 27 G5
Haroldslea Dri. RH6 27 G5
Harrowsley Ct. RH6 27 F2
Harrowsley Green La. RH6 27 H4
Harvestside. RH6 27 F2
Hatchgate. RH6 26 D4
Hayfields. RH6 27 F2
Hazelhurst. RH6 27 G2
Heatherlands. RH6 27 F2
Hedingham Clo. RH6 27 G2
Heritage Lawn. RH6 27 F2
Heronswood Ct. RH6 27 F2
Hevers Av. RH6 26 D2
High St. RH6 27 E3
Hilton Ct. RH6 27 G2
Holmbury Keep. RH6 27 F2
Homefield Clo. RH6 27 F2
Honeysuckle Clo. RH6 27 G2
Hookwood Rd. RH6 26 B4
Horley Rd. RH6 26 A6
Horley Row. RH6 26 D2
Horse Hill. RH6 26 A3
Hurst Rd. RH6 26 C2
Hutchins Farm. RH6 26 D1
Hutchins Way. RH6 26 D1
Hyperion Walk. RH6 27 F5
Jennings Way. RH6 27 H3
Kelsey Clo. RH6 26 D3
Kidworth Clo. RH6 26 D1
Kiln La. RH6 26 D1
Kimberley Clo. RH6 26 D3
Kings Rd. RH6 27 E3
Kingsley Clo. RH6 26 D1
Kingsley Rd. RH6 26 D1
Ladbroke Rd. RH6 27 E1
Lake La. RH6 27 G1
Lambyn Clo. RH6 27 G2
Landen Pk. RH6 26 C1
Langshott. RH6 27 F1
Langshott La. RH6 27 F2
Larksfield. RH6 27 F2
Le May Clo. RH6 27 E2
Lechford Rd. RH6 27 E4
Lee St. RH6 26 C2
Limes Av. RH6 27 F4
Lincoln Clo. RH6 27 E4
London Rd. RH6 26 D5
Longbridge Gate. RH6 26 D6
Longbridge Rd. RH6 26 D5
Longbridge Walk. RH6 26 D5
Longchamp Clo. RH6 27 G3
Lumley Ct. RH6 27 E2
Lumley Rd. RH6 27 E2
Malcolm Gdns. RH6 26 B5
Mallards Clo. RH6 27 E1
Manor Clo. RH6 26 D3
Manor Dri. RH6 26 D3
Massetts Rd. RH6 26 D4
Mazecroft. RH6 27 F2
Meadowcroft Clo. RH6 27 G5
Meadowside. RH6 27 F2
Meathgreen Av. RH6 26 D1
Meathgreen La. RH6 26 C1
Meridian Gro. RH6 27 G2
Michael Cres. RH6 27 E5
Middlefield. RH6 27 G3
Mill Clo. RH6 26 C2
Mill La. RH6 26 B3
Mosford Clo. RH6 26 D1
Newlands Clo. RH6 26 D1
Norfolk Clo. RH6 27 E4
North Way. RH6 26 D6
Northgate Rd. RH6 26 D6
Oaklands. RH6 27 G3
Oakside Ct. RH6 27 G2
Oakside La. RH6 27 G2
Oakwood Rd. RH6 27 E2
Oatlands. RH6 27 F2
Oldfield Clo. RH6 26 D5
Oldfield Rd. RH6 26 D4
Orchard Clo. RH6 26 D2
Palmer Clo. RH6 26 C1
Park Lawn Av. RH6 26 D1
Park View. RH6 27 E2
Parkhurst Gro. RH6 26 D2
Parkhurst Rd. RH6 26 C2
Parkway. RH6 27 E3
Parsons Clo. RH6 26 C2
Perimeter Rd Nth. RH6 27 E6
Pine Gdns. RH6 27 E4
Povey Cross Rd. RH6 26 C5
Powell Clo. RH6 26 C2
Poynes Rd. RH6 26 C1
Primrose Av. RH6 27 F4
Priory Clo. RH6 26 D2
Queens Rd. RH6 27 E3
Racecourse Way. RH6 26 D6
Ramsey Clo. RH6 26 D3
Raymer Walk. RH6 27 G2
Reigate Rd. RH6 26 A1
Rickwood. RH6 27 F2
Ringley Av. RH6 27 E3
Riverside. RH6 27 E5
Roffey Clo. RH6 26 D3
Rosemary Ct. RH6 26 C2
Rosemary La. RH6 27 F3
Rudgwick Keep. RH6 27 F2
Russells Cres. RH6 27 E4
Russet Clo. RH6 27 G3
Rutherwick Clo. RH6 26 D3
Ryelands. RH6 27 F2
St Georges Rd. RH6 27 F3
St Hildas Clo. RH6 27 E2
Sangers Dri. RH6 26 D3
Sarel Way. RH6 27 E1
Saxley. RH6 27 G2
Silverlea Gdns. RH6 27 F4
Skipton Way. RH6 27 E1
Smallfield Rd. RH6 27 F3
Smallmead. RH6 27 F3
Smithbarn Clo. RH6 27 F1
South Parade. RH6 26 D2
Southlands Av. RH6 26 D2
Spiers Way. RH6 27 F5
Staffords Pl. RH6 27 F5
Station App. RH6 27 F3
Station Rd. RH6 27 F3
Stockfield. RH6 27 F2
Stocks Clo. RH6 27 F4
Stonecourt Clo. RH6 27 G3
Suffolk Clo. RH6 27 E4
Tanyard Way. RH6 27 F1
Tarham Clo. RH6 26 C1
Thatchers Clo. RH6 27 F1
The Avenue. RH6 26 D4
The Close. RH6 27 G5
The Coronet. RH6 27 G5
The Crescent. RH6 27 E5
The Dell. RH6 27 F2
The Drive. RH6 27 E4
The Fieldings. RH6 27 F2
The Glebe. RH6 26 D3
The Grove. RH6 27 F4
The Meadway. RH6 27 F3
The Ridgeway. RH6 27 E5
The Spinney. RH6 27 E1
Thornton Clo. RH6 26 D3
Thornton Pl. RH6 26 D3
Todds Clo. RH6 26 C1
Tower Clo. RH6 26 D3
Twyner Clo. RH6 27 G2
Upfield. RH6 27 E4
Upfield Clo. RH6 27 E5
Vicarage La. RH6 26 D2
Victoria Clo. RH6 27 E3
Victoria Rd. RH6 27 E3
Waritersville Way. RH6 27 G5
Waterside. RH6 27 E1
Wellington Way. RH6 26 D1
Wesley Clo. RH6 27 E1
West Leas. RH6 26 C1
West Mead. RH6 27 G3
Westcott Keep. RH6 27 F2
Wheatfield Way. RH6 27 F1
Whitecroft. RH6 27 F2
Whithey Mdws. RH6 26 B5
Whitmore Way. RH6 26 C2
Wickham Clo. RH6 26 D2
Willow Brean. RH6 26 C1
Windmill Clo. RH6 27 F3
Wither Dale. RH6 26 C1
Withey Brook. RH6 26 B5
Wolverton Clo. RH6 26 D5
Wolverton Gdns. RH6 26 D4
Woodcote. RH6 27 F2
Woodhayes. RH6 27 F2
Woodroyd Av. RH6 26 D4
Woodroyd Clo. RH6 26 D5
Wysemead. RH6 27 G2
Yattendon Rd. RH6 27 F3
Yew Tree Clo. RH6 26 D1

LEATHERHEAD & DORKING AREAS

Abinger Clo. RH5 24 C5
Adlers La. RH5 22 A5
Admirals Rd. KT23 3 F3
Agates La. KT21 5 H1
Albany Park Rd. KT22 5 E1
Allen Rd. KT23 3 D3
Amey Dri. KT23 3 E2
Ansell Rd. RH4 23 B3
Aperdele Rd. KT22 4 C2
Apple Tree Clo. KT22 3 E1
Arbour Clo. KT22 4 D5
*Archway Mews, Meadowbrook Rd. RH4 23 A3
Arundel Rd. RH4 23 A4
Ashcombe Rd. RH4 23 A2
Ashdale. KT23 3 E3
Ashley Clo. KT23 3 B3
Ashley Rd. RH4 24 B2
Ashwood Pk. KT23 3 E1
Atwood. KT23 3 A1
Back Alley. RH4 23 B4
Badingham Dri. KT22 4 C5
Bailey Rd. RH4 24 B2
Barclay Clo. KT22 4 A5
Barley Mow Ct. RH3 25 C2
Barn Meadow La. KT23 3 B1
Barnett Clo. KT22 5 F1
Barnett Wood La. KT22 5 F2
Barrett Rd. KT22 3 F2
Barrington Rd. RH4 23 A5
Bay Tree Av. KT22 5 F2
Beales Rd. KT23 3 D4
Beattie Clo. KT23 3 B1
Beckley Par. KT23 3 E3
Beech Clo. RH4 23 A3
Beech Gro. KT23 3 C4
Beech Holt. KT22 5 G4
Beechwood Park. KT22 5 G4
Bell La. KT22 4 C5
Bell Lane Clo. KT22 4 C5
Belmont Rd. KT22 5 E4
Bennetts Farm Pl. KT23 3 B2
Bentsbrook Clo. RH5 24 B5
Bentsbrook Park. RH5 24 B5
Bentsbrook Rd. RH5 24 B5
Beresford Rd. RH4 23 B4
Bickney Way. KT22 4 A4
Bilton Centre Pk. KT22 5 E2
*Bishops Cottages, Reigate Rd. RH3 25 A1
Blackbrook Rd. RH5 24 D4
Blackthorne Rd. KT23 3 E3
Blades Clo. KT21 5 H2
Blind La. RH3 25 C5
Boleyn Walk. KT22 5 E2
Bookham Gro. KT23 3 D3
Bourne Gro. KT21 5 H1
Boxhill Way. RH3 25 B6
Bracken Clo. KT23 3 B1
Bradley La. RH5 22 A6
Brewhouse Rd. RH3 25 B6
Bridge St. KT22 5 E4
Brockham Grn. RH3 25 B3
Brockham La. RH3 25 A1
Broderick Gro. KT23 3 C3
Brook Clo. RH4 23 C2
Brook Way. KT22 4 B2
Broomfield Park. RH4 24 B2
Browning Rd. KT22 3 F2
Brympton Clo. RH4 23 A6
Buffers La. KT22 5 F1
Bull Hill. KT22 5 F3
Burney Clo. KT22 3 E2
Burney Rd. RH5 22 A5
Burnhams Rd. KT23 3 A1
Burrows Clo. KT23 3 B1
Bushbury La. RH3 25 A6
Bushey Shaw. KT21 4 D1
Bushy Rd. KT22 4 A4
Byron Pl. KT22 5 F4
Byttom Hill. RH5 22 C3
CaenWood Rd. KT21 4 D2
Calvert Cres. RH4 23 B2
Calvert Rd. RH4 23 B2
Camilla Clo. KT23 3 D2
Camilla Dri. RH5 22 A4
Candy Croft. KT23 3 D3
Cannon Gro. KT22 4 C4
Cannon Way. KT22 4 C3
Cannonside. KT22 4 C4
Cedar Ct. RH4 23 B4
Cedar Dri. KT22 4 D5
Chalkpit La. RH3 25 B1
Chalkpit La. RH4 23 A3
Chalkpit Ter. RH4 23 A2
Challenge Ct. KT22 5 F1
Chantrey Clo. KT21 5 H1
Chapel Clo. RH4 23 A3
Chapel La. RH4 24 A2
Chapel La. RH5 22 A5
Chardhurst Clo. RH5 24 D4
Charlwood Clo. KT23 3 D1
Chart Clo. RH5 23 C6
Chart Downs. RH5 24 C4
Chart La. RH4 23 B4
Chart La Sth. RH5 23 C5
Chequers Yd. RH4 23 A4
Cherkley Hill. KT22 22 C2
Chester Clo. RH4 23 C2
Chichester Clo. RH4 23 B2
Chichester Rd. RH4 23 B1
Childs Hall Clo. KT23 3 B3
Childs Hall Dri. KT23 3 B2
Childs Hall Rd. KT23 3 B2
Chilmans Dri. KT23 3 D3
Christie Clo. KT23 3 B3
Christy La. KT23 3 D3
Church Clo. KT22 3 F1
Church Gdns. RH4 23 B3
Church Rd. KT23 3 B1
Church Rd. KT22 5 F4
Church St. RH3 25 D3
Church St. RH4 23 A4
Church St. KT22 5 F4
Church Walk. KT22 5 F4
Churchill Clo. KT22 4 C5
Clandon Mews. RH4 24 A4
Clare Cres. KT22 4 C2
Clare Wood. KT22 4 C2

St Brelades Clo. RH4 23 A6
St Johns. RH5 24 B5
St Johns Av. KT22 5 F3
St Johns Clo. KT22 5 G2
St Johns Rd. KT22 24 A2
St Johns Rd. KT22 5 G3
St Martins Mews. RH4 23 A4
St Martins Pl. RH4 23 A3
St Marys Clo. KT22 4 C5
St Marys Rd. KT22 5 F4
St Nicholas Av. KT23 3 D2
St Nicholas Hill. KT22 5 G4
St Pauls Rd East. RH4 23 B4
St Pauls Rd West. RH4 23 A5
Salvation Pl. KT22 5 E6
Sandes Pl. KT22 4 C2
Sayers Clo. KT22 3 E1
School La. KT22 4 C4
School La. RH5 22 C3
School La. RH4 24 B2
Shamrock Clo. KT22 4 C3
Sharon Clo. KT23 3 C1
Shellwood Clo. RH5 24 C5
Shere Clo. RH5 24 C5
Sheridans Rd. KT23 3 E3
Sherwood Clo. KT22 4 B5
Shires Clo. RH1 5 H1
Silverdale Clo. RH3 25 B5
Sole Farm Av. KT23 3 B2
Sole Farm Clo. KT23 3 B2
Sole Farm Rd. KT23 3 B2
Solecote. KT23 3 C2
Sondes Place Dri. RH4 24 D1
South Dri. RH5 23 C4
South End. KT23 3 D3
South St. RH4 23 A5
South Ter. RH4 23 B5
South View Rd. KT21 5 H1
Southey Ct. KT23 3 D2
Spital Heath. RH5 23 C3
Spook Hill. RH5 24 B6
Spring Gdns. RH4 23 A3
Spring Gro. KT23 3 D1
Springfield Rd. RH4 24 A2
Squirrels Grn. KT23 3 C1
Station App. RH4 23 B2
Station App. KT23 3 C1
Station Rd. RH3 25 D1
Station Rd. RH4 23 A4
Station Rd. KT22 5 E3
Stone Hill Clo. KT23 3 C2
Stones La. RH4 24 A2
Stubbs Clo. RH4 23 C6
Stubbs Hill. RH4 24 C4
Styles End. KT23 3 D4
Summerfield. KT21 5 H1
Sumner Clo. KT22 3 F2
Sunmead Clo. KT22 5 E4
Swan Ct. KT22 5 E3
Swan Mill Gdns. RH4 23 C2
Swanns Meadow. KT23 3 C3
Swanworth La. RH5 22 B3
Sycamore Clo. KT22 4 D4
Taleworth Pk. KT21 5 H2
Taleworth Rd. KT21 5 H1
Tanners Dean. KT22 5 H4
Tanners Hill. RH3 25 A3
Tanners Meadow. RH3 25 B6
Tate Clo. KT22 5 G5
Teatle Wood Hill. KT22 4 A1
Teazlewood Park. KT22 4 B1
Ten Acres. KT22 3 F2
Ten Acres Clo. KT22 3 F2
The Approach. KT23 3 B1
The Avenue. RH3 25 A2
The Ballands Nth. KT22 4 C4
The Ballands Sth. KT22 4 C5
The Beeches. KT22 4 D6
The Berkeleys. KT22 4 D6
The Blackburn. KT23 3 B2
The Borough. RH3 25 A3
The Burrell. RH4 24 A2
The Chine. RH3 23 B3
The Close. RH3 25 B6
The Copse. KT22 4 A5
The Crescent. KT22 5 F4
The Downs. KT22 22 C1
The Driftway. KT22 5 G5
The Drive. KT22 4 D4
The Fairway. KT22 4 C2
The Garstons. KT23 3 C2
The Glade. KT22 4 A4
The Green. KT22 3 F2
The Hildens. RH4 24 A3
The Knoll. KT22 5 G3
The Limes. KT22 5 G4
The Lorne. KT23 3 C3
The Moorings. KT23 3 C2

The Mount. KT22 4 D5
The Murreys. KT21 5 H1
The Orchard. RH5 24 C5
The Paddock. RH4 24 A2
The Paddocks. KT23 3 D3
The Park. KT23 3 C1
The Pines. RH4 23 B5
The Priors. KT21 5 H1
The Ridge. KT22 3 F1
The Ridgeway. KT22 4 C5
The Smithers. RH3 25 B4
The Spinney. KT23 3 D2
The Street. RH3 25 D2
The Street. KT22 4 B3
The Terrace. RH5 23 C5
The Twitten. RH4 5 H2
The Walled Gdn. RH3 25 D3
The Withies. KT22 5 G2
Thorncroft Dri. KT22 5 F5
Tilehurst La. RH5 23 D5
Timber Clo. KT23 3 E4
Tollgate Rd. KT22 23 B6
Tower Hill. RH4 23 B6
Tower Hill Rd. RH4 23 B6
Townfield Rd. RH4 23 A5
Townshott Clo. KT23 3 C3
Trasher Mead. RH4 23 C6
Treelands. RH5 24 C4
Tregarthen Pl. KT22 5 G3
Tudor Clo. KT23 3 C2
Tudor Walk. KT22 5 E2
Turville Ct. KT23 3 D3
Tweed La. RH3 25 A6
Twelve Acre Clo. KT23 3 B1
Tynedale Rd. RH3 5 H2
Uplands. KT21 5 H2
Upper Fairfield Rd. KT22 5 F3
Upper Rose Hill. RH4 23 B4
Vaughan La. RH4 23 A4
Vicarage Clo. KT23 3 C3
Vicarage La. KT22 5 F4
Victoria Ter. RH4 23 A4
Vincent Clo. KT23 3 D1
Vincent Dri. RH4 23 A5
Vincent La. RH4 23 A4
Vincent Rd. RH4 23 A4
Vincent Walk. RH4 23 A4
Wallis Mews. KT22 5 E4
Walford Rd. RH4 24 B5
Warren Rd. KT22 4 B5
Warrenne Rd. RH3 25 B4
Water La. KT23 3 A3
Waterfields. KT22 5 F1
Waterway Rd. KT22 5 E4
Wathen Rd. RH4 23 B3
Watson Rd. RH4 24 B2
Waverley Pl. KT22 5 H1
Wellhouse Rd. RH3 25 C5
Wells Clo. KT23 3 E2
West Bank. RH4 23 A5
West Down. KT23 3 D4
West Farm Av. KT21 5 H1
West Farm Clo. KT21 5 G1
West Farm Dri. KT21 5 H1
West St. RH4 23 A4
Westcott Mews. RH4 24 A2
Westcott Rd. RH4 24 C2
Westcott St. RH4 24 A2
Westhumble St. RH5 22 B5
Westlees Clo. RH5 24 C4
Wheelers La. RH3 25 B4
White Way. KT23 3 D3
Wildcroft Dri. RH5 24 C5
Willow Grn. RH5 24 B5
Willow Mead. RH4 23 A3
Willow Vale. KT22 4 A5
Windfield. KT22 5 G3
Windmill Dri. KT22 5 G5
Wonham La. RH3 25 D3
Woodbridge Av. KT22 4 C2
Woodbridge Gr. KT22 4 C2
Woodend. KT22 5 G6
Woodside. KT22 4 A4
Woodvill Rd. KT22 5 F2
Worple Rd. KT22 5 F4
Yarm Ct Rd. KT22 5 G5
Yarm Way. KT22 5 H3
Yeomans Croft. KT23 3 C3
Yew Tree Rd. RH4 23 A2
Young St. KT22 5 E6
Zig Zag Rd. RH5 22 C4

REIGATE & REDHILL AREA

Abbotts Rise. RH1 19 G1

Abinger Dri. RH1 19 F6
Albany Clo. RH2 18 B1
Albert Rd. RH1 17 E4
Albert Rd North. RH2 18 A2
Albert Rd South. RH1 18 A3
Albion Rd. RH2 18 C4
Albury Rd. RH1 17 E4
Alders Rd. RH2 18 C2
Alexander Rd. RH2 18 B6
Allingham Rd. RH2 18 B6
Alma Rd. RH2 18 C2
Alpine Rd. RH1 16 C6
Altdam Farm. RH1 21 G5
Althorne Rd. RH1 19 H5
Ambleside Rd. RH1 21 H3
Anglo Way. RH1 19 H2
Apley Rd. RH2 20 B1
Arbutus Clo. RH1 18 D6
Arbutus Rd. RH1 18 D6
Arden Clo. RH2 20 C2
Ardshiel Dri. RH1 19 F5
Ash Clo. RH1 17 E5
Ash Dri. RH1 19 H5
Ashcombe Rd. RH1 17 E2
Ashdown Clo. RH2 20 C2
Ashdown Rd. RH2 20 C2
Asylum Arch Rd. RH1 21 G1
Atherfield Rd. RH2 20 D1
Avenue Villas. RH1 17 E4
Back La. RH1 16 A4
Bancroft Ct. RH2 18 C4
Bancroft Rd. RH2 18 B4
Barons Way. RH2 20 B2
Battlebridge La. RH1 16 D5
Batts Hill. RH1 19 E2
Baxter Av. RH1 19 F3
Beaufort Clo. RH2 18 A3
Beaufort Rd. RH2 18 A3
Beaumonts. RH1 21 G6
Beech Dri. RH2 19 E3
Beech Rd. RH1 17 E1
Beech Rd. RH2 18 B1
Beehive Way. RH2 20 C2
Bell St. RH2 18 B4
Belmont Rd. RH2 18 D5
Beverley Heights. RH2 18 C1
Birchway. RH1 19 H5
Birkheads Rd. RH2 18 B2
Blackborough Clo. RH2 18 D4
Blackborough Rd. RH2 18 C4
Blackstone Clo. RH1 19 E4
Blackstone Hill. RH1 19 E4
Blackthorn Clo. RH1 19 E4
Blackthorn Rd. RH2 18 C6
Blanford Rd. RH2 18 C4
Bletchingley Clo. RH1 17 E4
Bletchingley Rd. RH1 17 E3
Bolsover Gro. RH1 17 G4
Bonehurst Rd. RH1 21 G6
Bourne Rd. RH1 17 E5
Bramble Clo. RH1 19 H5
*Bramble Walk,
    Bramble Clo. RH1 19 H5
Brambletye Park Rd.
    RH1 19 G6
Bramblewood. RH1 16 D4
Bramley Clo. RH1 19 F6
Brandsland. RH2 20 C2
Brightlands Rd. RH2 18 D2
Brighton Rd,
    Redhill, RH1 19 F5
Brighton Rd,
    Salfords. RH1 21 G5
Broadhurst Gdns. RH2 18 C6
Brokes Cres. RH2 18 B2
Brokes Rd. RH2 18 B2
Brook Rd,
    Merstham. RH1 17 E3
Brook Rd, Redhill. RH1 19 G3
Brookfield Clo. RH1 21 G3
Brooklands Ct. RH2 18 C2
Brooklands Way. RH1 19 F2
Brownlow Rd. RH1 19 F2
Buckhurst Clo. RH1 19 F2
Budgen Dri. RH1 19 G1
Burnham Dri. RH2 18 B3
Burwood Clo. RH1 19 G3
Bushetts Gro. RH1 16 D4
Bushfield Dri. RH1 21 H2
Caberfeigh. RH1 19 E3
Cambridge Sq. RH1 21 G1
Canada Rd. RH1 21 G2
Canada Dri. RH1 21 H2
Canons Clo. RH2 18 A2
Carlton Green. RH1 16 A6
Carlton Rd. RH1 19 F5
Carrington Clo. RH1 19 F3
Cartmel Clo. RH2 19 E2

Castle Clo. RH2 20 C2
Castle Dri. RH2 20 B2
*Castle Walk,
    London Rd. RH2 18 B3
Castlefield Rd. RH2 18 B3
Cavendish Gdns. RH1 19 H3
Cavendish Rd. RH1 19 G3
Caxton Rise. RH1 19 H3
Cedar Clo. RH2 18 D6
Chaldon Clo. RH1 19 F6
Chanctonbury Chase.
    RH1 19 H4
Chapel Rd. RH1 19 G3
Charman Rd. RH1 19 F3
Chart La. RH2 18 C4
Chart Way. RH2 18 C3
Chartfield Rd. RH2 18 C4
Cherry Green Clo. RH1 19 H5
Chesterton Dri. RH1 17 G3
Chestnut Clo. RH1 19 H5
*Chestnut Mead,
    Oxford Rd. RH1 19 F3
Chilberton Dri. RH1 17 E5
Chilmark Gdns. RH1 17 G3
Chipstead Clo. RH1 19 G5
Church Ct. RH2 18 C3
Church Hill. RH1 17 E1
Church Rd. RH1 19 F5
Church Rd. RH2 18 B6
Church St. RH2 18 B4
Church Walk. RH2 18 C4
Churchfield Rd. RH2 18 A3
Claremont Rd. RH1 16 C6
Clarence Rd. RH1 18 D6
Clarence Walk. RH1 19 E6
Clarendon Rd. RH1 19 G3
Clarendon Rd Sth. RH1 19 G2
Clayhall La. RH2 18 A6
Cleeves Ct. RH1 19 G2
Clyde Clo. RH1 19 H3
Cockshot Hill. RH2 18 C5
Cockshot Rd. RH2 18 C5
Colebrook Rd. RH2 19 F2
Colesmead Rd. RH1 16 B5
College Cres. RH1 16 D6
Colley Way. RH2 18 A1
Colman Way. RH1 16 A6
Common Rd. RH1 19 F6
Coneyberry Rd. RH2 20 D2
Conifer Clo. RH2 18 B2
Coniston Way. RH1 19 H3
Copley Clo. RH1 19 F1
Coppice La. RH1 19 A2
Copse Rd. RH1 18 D6
Copsleigh Av. RH1 21 G5
Copsleigh Clo. RH1 21 G4
Copsleigh Way. RH1 21 G4
Cornfield Rd. RH2 18 D5
Cotland Acres. RH1 19 E6
Crakell Rd. RH2 18 D4
Cranston Clo. RH2 18 C5
Crescent Rd. RH2 18 B6
Cromwell Rd. RH2 19 G3
Cronks Hill. RH1 18 D5
Cronks Hill Clo. RH1 19 E6
Cronks Hill Rd. RH1 19 E5
Crossland Rd. RH1 19 H3
Crossways La. RH1 16 A3
Croydon Rd. RH2 18 C3
Daneshill. RH1 19 F2
Daneshill Clo. RH1 19 F2
Deans Rd. RH1 17 E5
Deerings Rd. RH2 18 B6
Delabole Rd. RH1 16 D4
Delamere Rd. RH2 20 C2
Dennis Clo. RH1 19 F1
Denton Clo. RH1 21 G1
Devon Cres. RH1 19 E4
Devon Rd. RH1 17 E5
Diamond Ct. RH1 19 F3
Dome Way. RH1 19 F3
Doods Park Rd. RH2 18 C3
Doods Rd. RH2 18 D3
Doods Way. RH2 18 D3
Doran Dri. RH1 19 E3
Douglas Rd. RH2 18 C3
Dovers Green Rd. RH2 20 C3
Downswood. RH1 16 A6
Duncroft Clo. RH2 18 A3
Dundrey Cres. RH1 17 G3
Dunlin Clo. RH1 21 F3
Dunottar Clo. RH1 19 E6
Dunraven Av. RH1 21 H5
Durfold Dri. RH2 18 D3
Earlsbrook Rd. RH1 19 G5
Earlswood Rd. RH1 19 F5
East Rd. RH2 18 A3
East Walk. RH2 18 C3

Eastnor Rd. RH2 18 B6
Edgefield Clo. RH1 21 H3
Effingham Rd. RH2 18 C4
Eldersley Clo. RH1 19 F1
Eldersley Gdns. RH1 19 F1
Elm Rd. RH1 19 F4
Elmwood Rd. RH1 16 D5
Emlyn Rd. RH1 19 G5
Endsleigh Rd. RH1 17 E4
Eversfield Rd. RH2 18 C3
Evesham Clo. RH2 18 A3
Evesham Rd. RH2 18 A3
Evesham Rd Nth. RH2 18 A3
Fairfax Av. RH1 19 F3
Fairford Clo. RH2 18 D2
Fairhaven Rd. RH1 16 C5
Fairlawn Dri. RH1 19 E5
Felland Way. RH2 20 D2
Feltham Rd. RH1 21 F3
Feltham Walk. RH1 21 F3
Fengates Rd. RH1 19 F3
Fenton Clo. RH1 19 G3
Fenton Rd. RH1 19 G3
Fir Tree Walk. RH2 18 D4
Flint Clo. RH1 19 F2
Fountain Rd. RH1 19 F5
Fox La. RH2 18 C1
Foxley Clo. RH1 21 H3
Frenches. RH1 19 G1
Frenches Ct. RH1 19 G1
Frenches Rd. RH1 16 D6
Friths Dri. RH2 18 C1
Fulbourne Clo. RH1 19 F1
Furze Clo. RH1 19 F3
Furze Hill. RH1 19 F3
Furzefield Cres. RH2 18 D5
Furzefield Rd. RH2 18 D5
Gable Ct. RH1 19 G3
Garibaldi Rd. RH1 19 F4
Garlands Rd. RH1 19 F4
Gatton Bottom. RH1 16 B2
Gatton Clo. RH2 18 D1
Gatton Park Rd. RH1 16 A6
Gatton Rd. RH2 18 D1
Gloucester Rd. RH1 19 G2
Glovers Rd. RH2 18 C5
Goodwood Rd. RH1 19 F2
Gordon Rd. RH1 16 D6
Grange Clo. RH1 19 E1
Grange Dri. RH1 17 E3
Grantwood Clo. RH1 21 H3
Green La, Redhill. RH1 19 E1
Green La, Reigate. RH2 18 A4
Green La,
    White Bushes. RH1 21 H3
Green Way. RH1 19 F3
Greenhayes Clo. RH2 18 D3
Greensand Rd. RH1 17 F3
Greenwood Dri. RH1 21 H3
Greystones Clo. RH1 18 D6
Greystones Dri. RH2 18 D1
Grosvenor Mews. RH2 20 C1
Grovehill Rd. RH1 19 F3
Gurneys Clo. RH1 19 G4
Haigh Cres. RH1 19 H5
Hampton Rd. RH1 21 G3
Hanover Clo. RH1 17 E3
Hanworth Rd. RH1 21 F3
Hardwick Rd. RH1 18 D6
Hardwicke Rd. RH2 18 B3
Harewood Clo. RH1 18 D1
Harrison Clo. RH2 18 C5
Hartington Pl. RH2 18 B2
Hartspiece Rd. RH1 19 H5
Hartswood Av. RH2 20 B2
Hatchlands Rd. RH1 19 E3
Hawthorn Clo. RH1 21 H3
Hawthorn Wa. RH1 19 H5
Hazel Clo. RH1 21 H3
Hazel Rd. RH2 18 C6
Heather Clo. RH1 16 D5
Heathfield Dri. RH1 21 F2
Heston Rd. RH1 21 F2
Heston Walk. RH1 21 F2
Hethersett Clo. RH2 18 D1
High Dri. CR5 16 A1
High St,
    Merstham. RH1 17 E3
High St, Redhill. RH1 19 G3
High St, Reigate. RH2 18 B4
High Trees Rd. RH2 18 D5
Highlands Rd. RH2 19 E3
Hildenly Clo. RH1 17 F3
Hill House Dri. RH1 18 C6
Hillfield Clo. RH1 19 H3
Hillfield Rd. RH1 19 H3
Hilford Pl. RH1 21 G4
Hilltor Rd. RH2 18 C5